T0114615

MEDITATION,
THE PHYSICAL BODY

ELIZABETH BANFALVI

BALBOA.PRESS
A DIVISION OF HAY HOUSE

Balboa Press books may be ordered through booksellers or by contacting:

Balboa Press
A Division of Hay House
1663 Liberty Drive
Bloomington, IN 47403
www.balboapress.com
844-682-1282

Print information available on the last page.

ISBN: 979-8-7652-3227-9 (sc)
ISBN: 979-8-7652-3228-6 (e)

Balboa Press rev. date: 07/26/2022

Also by Elizabeth Banfalvi

Meditation Series:
Meditation: The Physical Body
Meditation: Awareness
Meditation: Relaxation
Meditation: The Hectic Life
Meditation: The Mental Life
Meditation: Defining your Space
The Little Book of Meditation
The Little Book of Breathing
The Little Book of Stress

Meditation
The Physical Body

To Be – You Have to Know,
Accept and Acknowledge

CONTENTS

INTRODUCTION

If you look up meditation in the dictionary, the meaning is simply to focus. It is about taking a moment in time and focusing on a thought, an action, a thing or nothing at all. To meditate is to discover who you are physically, mentally and spiritually. It enables you to take a step back and be alone with yourself. It is about peeling off the "should/coulds", the "wants/desires" and the "(im)perfections".

Meditation is very natural and we do actually know how to meditate. It is when we let go and enjoy a scene, read, laugh or focus completely. The problem starts when we cannot do these simple things and our minds cannot focus.

I have been teaching meditation for many years and the students that come into my class for the first time look for relaxation. They confess they cannot focus or their minds are too active to relax. It is difficult for them to just sit and relax and stop holding onto their stress.

Some new students think meditation is a metaphysical practice of sitting quietly for a certain amount of time in a lotus position and making funny breathing noises. Students want to know how to begin meditating and to incorporate it into their everyday life. I help them realize they don't have to dedicate large amounts of time to meditate to get the feeling of relaxation. Even if they only take the time to focus their mind for a short time, learn some easy breathing exercises and be aware physically and mentally, they will be able to relax and focus.

So, I start them in the first classes on the physical journey of meditation to train the mind and body to work together. Your mind thinks stress thoughts so your body tenses. Your body is tight so your mind holds stress thoughts. There is a synchronicity between the mind and the body – when one relaxes then the other follows naturally.

In the first class, I always ask my students how they are feeling. Most cannot answer or are very vague about their answers because they find it hard to get in touch with their physical body. I prompt them with words such as warm/cool and/or tense/relaxed. I get them to acknowledge how they are feeling so they eventually begin to recognize the changes in their bodies. At the end of the meditations, I ask them again how they are feeling. So often I get the answers that they didn't realize they were so tense until they began to focus on their bodies and relax. Every class I make a point of asking them how they are feeling or get them involved in their evolution. At times they realize after I have asked them that changes have occurred. So often when they listen to others in the class, they realize that they also are having the same experiences of changes in their lives. Changes are sometimes subtle but once acknowledged they know happy changes are happening.

First, we start with the physical body and treat it like an exercise routine to get the body to respond. Repetition and routine are keys so that the body learns to "experience" the feeling of being relaxed. A chin tuck and pelvic tilt are some of the ways your body will relax naturally. I always incorporate sitting, laying and standing into the meditations to help the students realize that they don't need to be in one position to meditate. They learn that they can meditate anywhere or anyplace.

Secondly, the next aspect I suggest to my class is to journal. When you first begin to meditate, it is important to journal your progress. It is very important to log how you feel and the differences that are taking place within the body but also your mindset. Be specific on your entries so that you can read back on the changes taking place. Basically, you cannot change what you don't know exists. I make a point of the fact that when you journal, you bring more of an acknowledgement to how you feel because you have written it down. Thinking is one energy but writing it brings it into being and helps to make it a history of where you were at a certain point in time.

Acknowledge where the "differences" are within the body and mind. Basically, where do you feel the tension? What part of the body do you feel the most tension? Do you feel it in the back? Hands? Each person is unique and holds on to their tension differently and as you journal you begin to realize this and it becomes easier to begin to release or ease the tension.

This book will help you start the journey. It is kept very simple and helps train you to respond physically. It is written in point form so you can easily go from one point to the next. Each meditation and journal entry has a beginning, middle and end so they are complete. Do each section through in sequence initially and stay true to it as it is set out.

Once you have completed the meditations, go over them again and be aware of any changes or how different you feel. Acknowledge successes no matter how small they are. Be consistent in your time and place. Make a routine of how you approach these meditations so your response will be familiar and your body will begin to know it is time to meditate and relax.

As you go through the meditations and journal entries, pay attention to the ones that are easier and be aware of the ones which are more difficult. Repeat the difficult ones more often and push through until they feel comfortable and you are at ease with them.

Celebrate your accomplishments. This is about gaining insights about yourself and letting go of the unnecessary.

PRELIMINARIES

THE MEDITATIONS

1. Each of the meditations is in point form – follow them as they are set up. Do each of them in succession at least two times and then repeat the ones you like the best. Remember do the ones you don't like as much because usually there is more gained by pushing through what you don't like/want. Each meditation should eventually have a familiarity to you.

2. JOURNAL, JOURNAL AND JOURNAL some more. This will be your log of how you are feeling and how you are achieving what you want. Date and time each of your entries so you know how you have changed and progressed. It will amaze you.

3. Do the meditations to your own physical restrictions – do not overexert yourself – this is not about pain but about aligning yourself. As you repeat the same meditations, you will find that you will physically be able to do them because they will be familiar to you and you will be more relaxed.

4. Be consistent. When you first start the meditations, do them every day or at a consistent time span. Keep them to the same time of day and location so they will become familiar to you.

5. Make a routine of them. It is easier when the meditations become routine. Start at the same time, same location and similar clothing. Use the same equipment, mats, towels or cushions. It will become routine to you so that you just have to put on your clothes, unroll your mat and already you start to relax.

6. In the beginning, I would suggest the meditations be kept very simple, do not over stimulate. Keep it quiet and warm. Once you become familiar with the meditations, add music, candles, crystals, incense or whatever you would like to add. At first, do away with the distractions.

7. Do the meditations alone and at your own pace. Later if you want to do them with someone, go ahead. In the beginning, you want to establish yourself with the newness of what you are doing.

8. Once you are familiar with the meditations, try doing them at different times or locations. Get used to the idea that you can meditate anywhere and anytime even if you don't do the complete meditation. Pick what

you can do wherever you are and do it. If you sit in front of a computer, practice the "chin tuck" or "shoulder roll". It will help you relax and lessen the stress at the end of the day.

9. Never assume that you have to sit and meditate for a certain amount of time to accomplish the meditative way of life. That's a wonderful assumption but we don't always have the time. Take a few moments every day, sit back and do some of the exercises even just the breathing is great. I used to practice it on the commute each morning and evening because I knew I had a half hour each way to relax completely.

10. Teach your children or let children watch you and explain what you are doing if they ask. Teach them by practicing in front of them – get them to help you if they want but never force. Children learn more by actions than by words.

11. Keep your animals and plants nearby and let them help you relax. Both animals and plants add a dimension to your meditations by keeping nature close to you.

12. Do your meditations in nature even if it is just in front of a window or patio door. Go outside and do them in a forest, beside a stream, overlooking a beautiful scene, under the moonlight – nature adds a beautiful dimension to your meditations. Walk beside some trees or in a grassy area and think about how you feel when you meditate and you will feel more relaxed.

13. Take time for yourself every day to relax even if you don't do the meditations. Take some of the exercises with you and invent your own. Make it your own personal routine.

JOURNALING

Journaling is essential on our journey. Some people can make volumes of journals and others like me, can't. That is just the way it is. Some journaling is better than none and it gives you an idea of how you have changed and evolved.

In each part of our lives, we evolve and we would probably be surprised if we had made a journal of our lives as we lived it. What we were at 5, 15, 25, 35 and onwards is different than how we are now. Imagine how interesting it would be now if we knew what we felt or did at those times in our lives. Our recollections tend to change as time goes by and also the people that lived the memories with us. Each of us experiences the same memory differently.

Realize that in every moment we change. For example, think of deep new fallen snow and we walk in a large circle and come back to our own footsteps. Even in the time we took to go around the circle, we cannot follow our own footsteps through the snow. Everything changes us. Our environments, birthplace, heritage, traumas, friends/foes/parents/siblings/relatives/ strangers, etc. etc. have an effect on us.

Change is one of the constants in our lives. Our physical body changes on a molecular level at all times. Our blood is circulating, our breathing is constant, our food is digesting and on and on. Our nails and hair grow constantly. Changes surround us constantly.

So, in our lives there is also death or end so that something new will develop or has a chance to be born. We leave parts of ourselves behind. We end part of our childhood to begin school to grow in another direction. We leave or lose a job to begin another. At times we are forced by circumstances to change to end part of our familiarity to take a chance/ leap of faith to begin something new. Imagine how uninteresting our lives would be if this didn't happen. I know I have been taken kicking and screaming into some things that were more fulfilling than I could have ever imagined.

Life is about change about extending ourselves into the new and having the faith that either we find solid ground or we learn to fly. It is at times about survival about being forced to start over again when you are left with nothing but a feeling of emptiness.

5

These are the times you should journal your thoughts and feelings because in time it will show you how incredible your life has been. Beyond all the times in your life when you thought there was no hope or it couldn't get better, it does.

The Process

1. The date is where you begin. Date and time each entry.
2. State how you are feeling. So, how are you feeling – hot/cold/ warm, stressed/relaxed, disappointed, sad, happy? Write it down and then elaborated on it. I have included some journal pages that you can use or you can make your own.
3. Describe something that has happened to you lately and how did you feel or it made you feel.
4. Describe something that has made you feel grateful – anything! Always be grateful even if it is just a small thing, a person or event. Gratitude brings better things to your life.
5. End the entry with something that makes you happy. Find something! Have fun with them.

PRECAUTIONS

In everything in life, there are precautions. The caution is about exerting ourselves or doing something that isn't comfortable. Please pay attention to how you are feeling when you are doing the poses or the extensions.

1. Keep water close by. It helps with hydration and it also wakes the body after meditation and grounds it.
2. Keep warm by wearing layers – your body will tend to cool when you are relaxing and the extremities will be cooler because the energy will go more to the core of the body.
3. When stretching, go to your comfort level only. As you continue to practice the different meditations, you will be able to stretch further but at first, go only to your comfort level.
4. If you have been injured or have certain health conditions, adapt the movements to your comfort and imagine yourself going further. This will give you close to the same result but won't overextend yourself.
5. If you are weak in parts of your body, pay attention. At times, you will be asked to turn your head and if you have a neck injury, support the head and only rotate to your comfort.
6. If you need to balance yourself with a chair or a wall, do so.
7. If you are being asked to stretch your arms or legs out and you need support to keep them there, use a pillow, rolled up yoga mat, chair/stool, or wall to support you. Eventually, you will be able to do so without support but prevent injuries at all costs.
8. When you first begin taking deeper breaths, you may become dizzy. This is completely natural. Stop until the dizziness subsides and begin again.
9. With breathing exercises, your ribs will begin to be sore. You will be taking deeper breaths and your muscles surrounding your rib cage will expand because the lower lobes of your lungs are being filled. The muscles are being forced to stretch as you breathe deeper. The muscles will strengthen as you continue to breathe deeper.

10. When you take a breath and raise your breastbone up, this stretches out the muscles surrounding it. The muscles will stretch the more you do this and will reduce the stress across the back shoulder area.

11. When you are being asked to do standing poses, ensure your feet are planted firmly on the floor rather than on the sides or inner arch of the foot. This will keep you more balanced and prevent pressure on the sides of the feet and ankles.

12. In standing poses, ensure the knees are bent slightly and do not overextend the back of the legs. Keep the balance over the feet and ankles.

13. When asked to bend forward, go as far as comfortably possible or prop your arms on a chair if necessary. If you are being asked to keep the back straight, do so even if you don't go very far. Rotate from the hip and pelvis joints.

14. Be aware of the fact that we are either stiffer or tender on one side than the other. This again is completely natural.

15. You will find at times that being still will bring awareness of different promptings and actions. Relax through them and realize that in time these will also subside. The physical list, things to do, aches and pains will eventually subside.

16. When stretching or wiggling the toes, you may experience cramps but eventually they do subside when you are more relaxed and stretched out. Make sure you stretch before you begin and this will help.

17. During meditations, stronger feelings, memories and sensations may also surface. This is natural and it is important to remain relaxed. Journal your feelings and emotions. Don't ignore them but give them relevance and eventually you will work through them. It is time.

18. Your limitations will always change. Relax and do what you can. Imagine yourself as getting more flexible each time and that energy flows through you. The mind is powerful – use it.

THE POSES

There are natural positions and variations you can do to help the body relax. Be aware of how you stand, sit and lay and be very conscious about how your body feels. If you can follow some of these tips, you will be able to lessen your physical stress.

If you are very visual or even if you aren't, buy a book on anatomy. A book with lots of simple diagrams of the body showing the bones and muscles would really help when you are doing the meditations. There is so much on the internet now so check that out also. As you read the meditations, you can look at the pictures of the corresponding body parts. For example, if I am talking about the bones in the feet, you will be able to look at the diagrams and it will be easier to imagine them.

Below are the different terms and poses that are used. Do the preparations before starting the meditations and this will help to relax and prepare the body.

Common terms:

Arms and Legs Release – release the legs and arms to a good distance from the body – this releases the outer lateral muscles, the hip and shoulder joints. Put distance between the arm and armpit. This is where the lymph nodes are and this will help them function by releasing any pressure on them. Lymph nodes are part of the system that releases toxins from our body. **Breastbone Lift** – Lift the breastbone up to the ceiling. Lifting the breastbone raises the rib cage and the ribs are forced slightly forward. The shoulders drop back and down, and the breastbone muscles are stretched as opposed to the back shoulder area. Be careful not to overextend the curve of the back, tilt the pelvis slightly.

Chin Tuck – bring the chin to the breastbone and slowly release it back keeping the chin close to the breastbone – this releases the back neck and upper back shoulder muscles. Lead with your nose instead of your chin. This also aids in circulation to the head lessening headaches.

Head Roll/tilt – keeping the chin straight slowly roll/tilt the head to

9

the left and then to the right and back to the middle – this gives a rotation and a release to the neck joints and brings renewed circulation.

Palms & Soles – turn the palms upwards and release the fingers. Relax the soles of the feet by turning them slightly outwards. This opens your energy in both the feet and hands.

Pelvic Hand Tilt – while doing the laying pose, place your hands under the buttocks thumbs almost touching. This helps keep the pelvis tilted when you have to raise the legs or just lay quietly. It also helps to keep the back flat to the floor and not curved upwards.

Pelvic Tilt – tilt the pelvic area and pull the tummy muscles up towards the ribs – this supports the lower back and strengthens the tummy muscles and all the lower pelvic muscles. It also straightens the mid back and brings a rotation to the hip joints – all of this supports the lower and mid back.

Shoulder Roll – bring the shoulders blades together as much as possible then release them – this brings a rotation to the shoulder joints and releases stress across the upper back shoulder area. Keep the shoulder blades slightly tucked to support the spine.

Toes and Fingers – wiggle the fingers and toes and press each toe and finger into a surface – this releases tension, stress and stimulates energy.

Tummy Squeeze – Pull and then release the legs into the tummy area. This helps to massage the colon area and aids in digestion.

PREPARATIONS

Laying Pose

1. Lay comfortably in a warm and quiet room with either a mat or towel beneath you.
2. Release the legs and arms by spreading them away from the body and wiggle the fingers and toes.
3. Release the soles of the feet slightly outward and turn your palms upwards.
4. If your legs are straight, use a pillow or rolled up towel under your knees to release the knee and hip joints.
5. Tilt the pelvis and bring the curve of the back to the floor – release slightly. Roll the hips sideways one way and the other until the hips feel comfortable on the floor.
6. Pull your shoulder blades together and then release slightly to support your spine from touching the floor. Repeat till comfortable.
7. Roll the head and do a chin tuck – be aware of the contact of the head with the floor. Repeat until comfortable.
8. Bring the legs together and bend the knees and bring them up into the tummy area. Wrap your arms around the knees and pull your legs into the tummy area – repeat at least 3 times massaging the colon area.
9. Release one leg and then the other and release them into the original position. Be aware of your body in contact with the floor or the feeling of the warm earth beneath you.
10. When you are finished and ready to stand up, roll onto one side and bring the knees up to hip level. Rest for a moment and put one hand flat on the floor. Push up from your hand to prevent dizziness. Come up on your knees and put one foot in front and flat on the floor. Put both hands on your thigh and push up from this position.

Sitting Pose

1. Sit comfortably in a warm and quiet room on the floor or a firm chair.
2. If sitting on a chair, keep your feet flat on the floor or on a cushion so that your feet are flat. Your hips should be above the knee level. Use a firm cushion if needed. Keep the knees comfortably apart and the hands folded in your lap with palms facing upwards.
3. If sitting on the floor, either with your legs crossed or straight, keep the hip area elevated about 3 inches to help the back stay straight. Keep the hands comfortably in your lap with palms facing upwards.
4. Wiggle the fingers and toes. Spread the fingers and toes apart and then release.
5. Rock back and forth in your hip joints and on your buttock muscles.
6. Tilt the pelvis and feel the contact you have between your sitting bones and the chair or floor beneath you.
7. Raise the breastbone and the ribs will open. Your shoulders will also drop naturally, which will reduce stress.
8. Bend your elbows and bring them together behind your back, bringing your shoulder blades together as much as possible. Bring your elbows forward to touch in front. Repeat. Release the elbows and the shoulders will drop naturally.
9. Drop the arms as you turn or tilt the head from one side to the other slowly. Return the hands to the lap. Dropping the arms adds a slight stretch to the neck muscles.
10. Do a chin tuck.
11. Release the arms and bring yourself forward over the knees as much as you comfortably can and just sit bent over, arms hanging loosely till you feel the back relax. This massages the colon area.
12. Roll yourself up slowly to your sitting pose with your hands resting in your lap. Be aware of your sitting bones in contact with the chair or floor or the feeling of sitting on the warm earth.
13. When you are finished and are ready to stand, come up on your knees and place one foot in front, flat on the floor. Put both hands on your thigh and push up from this position.

Standing Pose

1. Stand comfortably in a warm and quiet room with your feet about a foot apart for balance.
2. Keep the feet facing forward and your arms comfortably at your sides.
3. Wiggle and stretch apart the toes and fingers. Shake your hands and legs to relax them.
4. Bend the knees comfortably and straighten them keeping a slight bend in them.
5. Rock back and forth in your hip joints and into your waist and rib area.
6. Tilt the pelvis area and tighten the tummy muscles – repeat several times and keep the pelvis slightly tilted.
7. Bend your elbows and bring them together behind your back bringing your shoulder blades together as much as possible. Bring your arms around the front and wrap them around you in a great big hug. Repeat several times alternating the position of the arms in the hug. Drop your arms comfortably at your sides when finished.
8. Keep the fingers and arms stretched downwards, do a head roll and chin tuck.
9. Stretch the legs further apart, keeping the knees bent and roll downwards between the legs. Let your arms and head hang. Stay as long as you comfortably can and then roll yourself up slowly. If this is uncomfortable, put your hands on a chair for support.
10. Assume the original position by bringing your feet a foot apart with arms comfortably at your sides. Keep your breastbone up, chin tucked and stand quietly for a moment. Imagine yourself standing in nature beneath a tree or on a beautiful mountain.

BREATHING EXERCISES

Much is written about the breath and the proper breathing and how important it is. It is very important because it helps the body replenish itself but also to keep it relaxed. Stop breathing for a couple of seconds and your body goes into trauma trying to get that next breath.

The breath also simulates how we feel. Short breaths simulate anxiety. Longer breaths simulate relaxation. We can use the breath to simulate the response we want. If we want to relax, slow the breath down and deepen it. If we need to get more energy, shorten the breath and do shorter breaths, inhaling through nose, exhaling through mouth.

Athletes are taught how to breathe properly to get the most affect out of their training. With a few tips we can all breathe deeper and keep more relaxed. Here are some pointers to consider:

Benefits of a longer deeper breath:

1. During sleep we breathe deeper because we are more relaxed
2. Alleviates headaches and fatigue
3. Relaxes nervous system, reduces stress and tension
4. Deep breathing massages and tones internal organs behind diaphragm muscle
5. Increases lung capacity and removes waste gas more efficiently from the lower lungs
6. Keeps lungs flexible and relaxed
7. Sighing/yawning means lack of oxygen within the body and is an automatic response
8. Deeper breath brings in more oxygen for purifying and rejuvenating the body

Posture (straight back allows the lungs to expand better):

1. Keep the back straight by raising the breastbone
2. Stretch the arms up raising the rib cage out of the waist
3. Sit straight with knees below hips – helps straighten the back

4. Stand straight with slight pelvic tilt – supports the lower back
5. Be relaxed – unclench hands and toes – open up

Nose vs. Mouth breathing:

1. Tiny hairs and mucous membranes in the nose filter out dust and toxins
2. The nose warms and humidifies the air for the lungs
3. The nasal system maintains the correct balance of oxygen and carbon dioxide in our blood
4. The mouth inhales and exhales air much quicker in large volumes leading to hyperventilation
5. The mouth doesn't clean or filter the air
6. The mouth is connected to the stomach and can lead to air flowing into the stomach and a limited amount going to the lungs

Pointers:

1. The lungs are made up of 3 lobes (parts) on the right and 2 on the left (room for the heart)
2. Pay attention to the breath and the movements of the body when inhaling
    a. Breastbone area are the top lobes – more anxious
    b. Upper rib cage are middle lobes
    c. Lower rib cage and abdominal area is the lowest lobe.
3. Readjusting the breath at first may result in anxiousness because the breath is the source of life and needs to be comforted. When holding the breath, the body might respond and feel anxious. This will fade as you become more practiced at doing the exercises and you feel more comfortable holding the breath.
4. When you start taking deeper breaths, your rib cage area will probably be sore. The soreness comes from the muscles surrounding the rib cage being stretched. This will fade but is a great indication that you are taking deeper breaths and working these muscles.
5. Always begin with a deep exhalation pulling in the tummy area to force the lower lungs to push out the air – exhalations should always

be longer than inhalations – allows for more flow of breath out of the body – lungs are one of the cleansing systems of the body.

6. Counting while you are breathing allows you to control the inhalation and exhalation and demonstrates how your breathing is changing when you can expand the count.

7. Inhale nose exhale nose for relaxation and rejuvenation.

8. Inhale nose exhale mouth for quick added energy.

BREATHING TECHNIQUES

1. Complete Breath
    a. inhale count 4; exhale count 8 initially and increase the exhalation count as you become more practiced
    b. the complete lung area and rib cage are used
    c. each level of lungs expands (upper/middle/lower)
    d. the counting helps with controlling the breath
2. Humming Breathing
    a. inhale nose exhale keeping the mouth closed and humming the breath out
    b. creates awareness of breath and sound
    c. more control on the exhalation
    d. breath vibrates at the back of throat and into lungs which creates warmth
    e. relaxes respiratory system
    f. helps in lengthening exhalation
3. Alternate Nostril Breathing
    a. Variations in alternative nostril breathing • Close left nostril – inhale and exhale right nostril. Close right nostril – inhale and exhale left nostril. Repeat going back and forth between the nostrils. • Close left nostril – inhale right, close right – exhale and inhale left. Close left – exhale and inhale right nostril. Repeat going back and forth between the nostrils.
    b. Benefits • Helps clear congestion • Balances right/left sides of the brain • Creates a feeling of contentment • Helps the mind focus • Helps control the breath

"GETTING TO KNOW ME"

Journal Date & Time:

_____

My names and nicknames?

_____

My names and nicknames?

_____

Male/female?

_____

Roles I play- parent/sibling/child?

_____

Marital status & children?

_____

My career/job?

_____

Health matters?

_____

How I am feeling?

_____

I am visual, perceptual, auditory, tactile?

_____

The symbols I like most – circle, square, triangle?

_____

If I could grant a wish for my parents, what would it be?

_____

I love music? What kind?

_____

My favourite colour is?

_____

My greatest accomplishment is?

_____

I love to dance?

_____

The part of the day I love most?

_____

If I could change one thing in my parents' lives, what would it be?

_____

If I was an animal, which one would I be and why?

_____

I am modern, traditional, wacky?

_____

My sense of humour is?

_____

I just won the lottery, beyond helping friends and family, I am going to?

_____

I only have 24 hours to live, what am I going to do first?

_____

The person who had the greatest impact on me?

_____

I am most grateful for?

_____

I like flowers? What kind?

_____

How many friends do I have?

_____

I wish upon a star for ....?

_____

What is the one thing my parents gave me that I am most proud of?

_____

THE MEDITATIONS

LAYING POSE – BEGINNING

1. Assume the Laying Pose and relax for a moment. Lay with your legs apart and your arms away from your body, your palms up and your chin tucked.
2. Breathing: Take 3 slow breaths, inhaling and exhaling lengthening your exhalations each time. Let your body relax more with each breath. Keep a rhythm as you breathe, feeling your chest expand and contract with each breath.
3. Toes: Bring your legs together and bring your attention to your toes. Wriggle the toes to loosen them up and rotate your ankles first one way and then another. Curl your toes very tightly and release. Repeat.
4. Toes & ankles: Point your toes then bring your toes up and extend your heels. Point the toes, roll them up and extend the heels. Rotate the feet at the ankle joints one way and then the other. Relax the feet.
5. Legs & hips: Place your feet flat on the floor and slowly swing your legs one side towards the floor then the other comfortably working the hip joint and outer thigh area. Repeat and relax.
6. Hips: Pull one leg up to your hip and then lower the foot flat on the floor again. Pull the other leg up to your hip and then lower the foot flat on the floor again. Repeat. Be aware of the vertical movement of the hip joints.
7. Body curl: Inhale, exhale and roll the body into a ball bringing the knees into the tummy area and the head towards the knees. Wrap the arms around the knees. Inhale release, exhale come into the ball again. Repeat.
8. Lower body: Release the legs down to the floor. Roll the lower body slowly to the left and then to the right. Repeat.
9. Arms: Straighten your arms at shoulder level. Inhale slowly and raise your arms straight up, palms facing each other. Exhale and lower the arms, palms facing outwards. Repeat.
10. Shoulder blades: Tuck the shoulder blades and release. Repeat 2 more times. Let the shoulder muscles support the spine from touching the floor.

11. Slowly inhale and tilt the chin towards the ceiling exhale and let the chin descend towards the breastbone. Repeat slowly. Feel the throat area open and relax.

12. Chin: Rock your head slowly to one side, straighten and then to the other side. Repeat slowly bringing your head to the straight position each time.

13. Face: Scrunch your face up as if you smell a foul odor, keeping it tight then release slowly. Repeat.

14. Mouth & jaw: Open your mouth and rock your lower jaw back and forth. Finish by pushing your tongue to the roof of your mouth and holding for a few seconds. The tongue pushed to the roof of the mouth helps the jaw release and relaxes.

15. Tummy squeeze: Finish off by raising your knees to your tummy area and wrapping your arms around them. Slowly rock to one side and then the other, repeating several times. Release one leg then the other.

16. Rest for several minutes before standing.

17. When you are finished and ready to stand up, roll onto one side and bring the knees up to hip level. Rest for a moment and put one hand flat on the floor. Push up from your hand to prevent dizziness. Come up on your knees and put one foot in front and flat on the floor. Put both hands on your thigh and push up from this position.

Date & Time

_____

How do I feel?

_____

How was my day?

_____

What did I accomplish today?

_____

Did I make myself happy today?

_____

What one thing am I grateful for today?

_____

Did I meditate today?

_____

Did I enjoy my day?

_____

Did I enjoy my meals?

_____

Did I take time for myself?

_____

Am I proud of myself?

_____

SITTING POSE – BEGINNING

1. Assume the sitting pose and relax a moment. Elevate your hips slightly with a book or a firm pillow. Sit with your hands in your lap palms facing upward. Keep your chin tucked.
2. Sitting bones: Sit with your back straight and slightly tilt the pelvis area forward. Feel the contact of your sitting bones with the surface beneath you.
3. Toes & legs: Straighten the legs and bring your attention to the toes and legs, inhale and curl the toes and stiffen the legs. Exhale release the toes and legs and feel them lengthen. Repeat and relax.
4. Back tilt (floor): If sitting on the floor, spread your legs apart. Place your fingers/hands on the floor between your legs or on your knees and keep the back straight. Sit forward on your sitting bones lifting them slightly from the floor. Inhale, sit up and then exhale lean forward keeping the back straight. Inhale, sit back, exhale and lean forward. Repeat several times. Bring your legs together and shake them. Sit back on your sitting bones.
5. Back tilt (chair): If sitting on a chair, spread your knees apart with your hands on your knees. Sit forward on your sitting bones by lifting them slightly and sitting back down again. Lean forward with a straight back between your knees. Inhale raise up, exhale lean forward. Repeat. Bring your legs together and shake them. Sit back on your sitting bones.
6. Chin: Inhale, exhale and drop your chin to your breastbone. Inhale and raise the chin. Repeat. Finish by keeping the chin slightly tucked.
7. Head tilt: Drop your arms to your side. Inhale, exhale and slowly tilt your head to one side and hold. Inhale raising the head and tilt to the other side. Repeat. Return the hands to the lap and keep the head straight with the chin slightly tucked.
8. Chin & neck: Slowly inhale, exhale and lower your chin to the breastbone curling your head down, rounding your back and tilting the pelvis forward. Inhale and raise your chin to the ceiling – use caution for your back neck area – and curve your back in and tilt the pelvis backwards. Repeat comfortably and relax.

9. Arms: Inhale and drop your arms towards the floor. Place your hands flat on the floor. Exhale and feel the arms getting longer and longer and your palms becoming flatter on the floor, stretching the muscles all the way up to the neck. Inhale release, exhale lengthen the arms. Repeat several times. Return your hands to your lap, palms facing upward.

10. Hands: Sit with your hands in your lap. Inhale, exhale and curl both hands into fists. Inhale, release and stretch your fingers as much as you can (great for arthritis but use with caution), exhale curl your hands into fists. Repeat several times.

11. Palm & thumb: Bring both hands up in front of your chest area. Inhale, exhale for 3 counts and push the thumb into the middle of the palm of the other hand. Inhale release, exhale and push in. Repeat 1 more time and then switch to do the other hand. This is great for upset or nervous stomach.

12. Tummy squeeze: Bring your legs up to your tummy and wrap your arms around your legs. Inhale, exhale and bring your body into a tight ball, pulling your legs into your body, release and inhale. Repeat.

13. Finish off by sitting comfortably. Inhale, exhale and slowly close your eyes. Inhale, open your eyes slowly and then close the eyes as you exhale. Repeat and sit for a few moments longer.

14. When you are finished and ready to stand, come up on your knees and place one foot in front, flat on the floor. Put both hands on your thigh and push up from this position.

Date & Time

_____

How do I feel?

_____

How was my day?

_____

What did I accomplish today?

_____

Did I make myself happy today?

_____

What one thing am I grateful for today?

_____

Did I meditate today?

_____

Did I enjoy my day?

_____

Did I enjoy my meals?

_____

Did I take time for myself?

_____

Am I proud of myself?

_____

STANDING POSE – BEGINNING

1. Stand comfortably, legs slightly apart, pelvis tilted slightly forward. Keep a chair close by to rest your hands on for balance. Do each of the stretches slowly and feel your body responding. Take 3 long slow deep breaths deepening them each time.

2. Balance: Close your eyes and feel the contact of your feet with the floor. Open your eyes and without lifting any part of your feet, rock forward to your toes and back to your heels. Rock sideways to the inside and then the outside of the feet. Again, close your eyes and feel if the contact of your feet with the floor is more balanced. Repeat and relax.

3. Feet & ankles: Lift one heel and push into the ball and toes of that foot. Repeat with the other foot stretching out the insteps and working the ankle joints. Repeat. Finish off by lifting each of your feet and rotating the ankle one way and then the other. Relax.

4. Knees & calves: Keep the feet flat on the floor bend and straighten the knees slightly and feel the stretch in the calves as well as the tightening of the thigh muscles. Be aware of the movement in the knee joints. Repeat and relax.

5. Hip joints: Keep the feet flat and bend one knee, working the hip joint and bending the other knee. Repeat the same on the other hip. Relax.

6. Tummy: Bring your attention to the tummy area. Suck in your tummy area and slowly curl the pelvic area forwards flattening the back, bringing the belly button to the spine. Release and push the pelvic area back curving the back inwards comfortably. Repeat. The working of the tummy and pelvic areas massages the colon area aiding digestion. Relax.

7. Rib cage: Keeping the feet flat, raise the arms comfortably and stretch the fingers up. Pull up on the rib cage area, and tilt the pelvis area forward. Twist at the waist turning the shoulders slowly to the right and then left. Keep the pelvis slightly tucked forward to protect the lower back. Relax.

8. Shoulders: Standing comfortably, slowly raise and stretch up one shoulder then release and lower. Repeat with the other shoulder.

Then raise both shoulders and slowly lower them. Pay attention to the movement in the shoulder joints. Repeat and relax.

9. Arms and shoulder joints: Roll the shoulder joints back and forth to loosen them. Tilting the pelvis, inhale and slowly raise the arms up to meet above the head palms facing up. Exhale reversing the palms and lowering the arms slowly. Repeat and relax.

10. Head turns: With arms hanging, slowly turn your head to one side and look over the shoulder. Turn slowly to the other direction and look over the shoulder. Repeat comfortably and pay attention to the movement and stretch in your neck muscles. Relax.

11. Chin & neck: Drop the chin down to the breastbone and raise the chin slowly 2 inches. Tilt the chin to the right, making a "U" movement and then the left. Lower and then raise the chin keeping it tucked. Repeat comfortably. Again, become aware of the movement in the neck and the stretch in the neck muscles. Relax.

12. Mouth & jaw: Open the mouth completely and move the lower jaw one way and then the other loosening up the jaw muscle. Close the mouth and circle the inside of the mouth with the tongue. Push the tongue to the roof of your mouth and hold. Open the mouth and stick the tongue down and out stretching the tongue completely. Release the tongue and close the mouth, teeth slightly apart. Relax and become aware of the feeling of freshness and renewed circulation to the face. Relax.

13. Finish off by standing straight, feet slightly apart, pelvis tilted slightly forward and chin tucked. Take a breath slowly in and out through your nostrils. Repeat 2 more times. Relax.

14. Stand for a few minutes longer and relax, inhaling and exhaling in your natural rhythm.

Date & Time

_____

How do I feel?

_____

How was my day?

_____

What did I accomplish today?

_____

Did I make myself happy today?

_____

What one thing am I grateful for today?

_____

Did I meditate today?

_____

Did I enjoy my day?

_____

Did I enjoy my meals?

_____

Did I take time for myself?

_____

Am I proud of myself?

_____

LAYING POSE – STRETCHING

1. Assume the Laying Pose and relax a moment. Lay with your palms up and your chin tucked. Release your arms and legs.

2. Breathing: Take 3 slow breaths inhaling and exhaling lengthening your exhalations each time. Let your body relax more with each breath. Imagine the breaths as waves of the ocean rolling in and out on the beach.

3. Toes & ankles: Bring your legs together and bring your attention to your toes. Wriggle them to loosen them up and rotate your ankles first one way and then another. Stretch each of the toes apart and release. Slowly exhale and point your toes and then reverse inhale and point your heels forward. Feel your legs stretching all the way up to your buttocks as you push the heels forward. Repeat exhaling and pointing toes and then inhaling and pushing the heels. Relax. Take a breath and relax your feet.

4. Legs & hip: Shake your legs all the way to your hip joint. Loosen the hip joints and feel the energy within the joint. Keeping the leg straight, inhale, exhale and stretch the legs by pulling the knee caps up into the thighs and stiffening the entire leg length. Release, inhale, exhale then pull the knee caps up stiffening the legs one more time. Release and shake the legs again and relax.

5. Legs: Place both hands under the buttock muscles to keep the back flat to the floor. Place the left foot flat on the floor. Inhale and raise the right leg straight up, exhale and point the toes to the ceiling. Release and lower the leg and place the right foot flat on the floor. Inhale, raise the left leg, exhale and point the toes. Release the left leg and repeat with each leg. Keep one foot flat on the floor while raising the other leg. Release the legs and hands and relax.

6. Pelvic area: Bring your attention to the pelvic and hip joint areas. Inhale, exhale and tilt the pelvis forward releasing the hip joint area. Inhale, release the tilt, exhale and tilt the pelvis area forward. Release and relax the pelvic and hip area.

7. Tummy squeeze: Bring your legs up and wrap your arms around your knees. Inhale, relax, exhale and pull your legs into the tummy area

and hold. Be aware of the rotation of your hip joints. Inhale, relax, exhale pull the knees in. Release your legs one at a time down to the floor and relax.

8. Body curl: Be aware of the curve of your back – do not overextend the small of your back. Inhale, exhale and curl forward flattening your back to the floor. Inhale and curve the back upwards. Exhale and curl forward into a ball, inhale and curve your back. Release and relax the back.

9. Fingers & wrists: Shake your arms up to your shoulder joints to loosen the arms and joints. Bend your elbow several times and end by shaking them out again. Wriggle your fingers and rotate your wrists one way and then the other. Relax.

10. Arms: Bring your arms to your sides. Place your hands on your thighs. Inhale, exhale and stretch the hands towards your toes slowly. Do not lift your back from the floor. Release, inhale, exhale and now stretch the arms. Raise the arms straight up to the ceiling. Inhale, exhale and stretch the arms up without lifting your back up. Repeat. Lower your arms to above your head and beside your ears. Open up your armpits and have your palms facing upwards. Inhale, exhale and stretch the arms up as carefully as you can, keeping the armpits open. Repeat. Lower the arms and relax.

11. Head area: Bring your awareness to the head, neck and scalp area. Slowly inhale, exhale and tuck your chin to your breastbone letting your upper back muscles stretch – hold. Inhale and roll the head all the way up opening up the throat area, exhale, bring the head down and tuck the chin and hold. Pay attention to the way the head feels as it rolls on the floor. Repeat slowly. Relax.

12. Jaw: Bring your awareness to the jaw area. Slowly inhale and open the jaw as far as you can, sigh the breath out as you close the jaw. Feel your jaw opening all the way up to the ear area. Repeat and then relax

13. Eyes: Bring your awareness to the eye area. Slowly inhale and raise the eyebrows very high, exhale and lower the eyebrows and eyelids closing the eyes. Repeat and then relax.

14. Face: Bring your awareness to the face. Slowly inhale and scrunch the face completely, exhale and relax the face. Repeat and then relax.

15. Assume the beginning pose and slowly take 3 long deep breaths relaxing more with each breath. Lay there for a few minutes just relaxing.
16. When you are finished and ready to stand up, roll onto one side and bring the knees up to hip level. Rest for a moment and put one hand flat on the floor. Push up from your hand to prevent dizziness. Come up on your knees and put one foot in front and flat on the floor. Put both hands on your thigh and push up from this position.

Date & Time

_____

How do I feel?

_____

How was my day?

_____

What did I accomplish today?

_____

Did I make myself happy today?

_____

What one thing am I grateful for today?

_____

Did I meditate today?

_____

Did I enjoy my day?

_____

Did I enjoy my meals?

_____

Did I take time for myself?

_____

Am I proud of myself?

_____

SITTING POSE – STRETCHING

1. Assume the Sitting Pose and relax a moment. Sit with your hands in your lap palms facing upward. Keep your chin tucked.

2. Breathing: Take 3 slow breaths inhaling and exhaling lengthening your exhalations each time. Let your body relax more with each breath. Close your eyes and relax.

3. Sitting bones: Be aware of your sitting bones on the floor or chair. Rock back and forth on your sitting bones to ensure balance. Keep the pelvis tucked slightly, feeling complete contact between the body and the floor.

4. Legs: Straighten your legs out in front of you. Shake your legs all the way up to your hip joint. Wiggle your toes and rotate the ankles one way and then the other.

5. Toes and heels: Inhale slowly and relax. Exhale and point your toes, stretching them forward rounding the top arch of your feet. Inhale bringing the toes up and extending the heels. Repeat exhaling pointing the toes and inhaling extending the heels. Repeat slowly and then relax the feet.

6. Buttocks: Inhale tensing the back of your legs and buttocks lifting your body slightly. Exhale slowly and relax. Repeat by inhaling and tensing the back of the legs, exhaling allowing the tenseness to release and flow out of your legs. Repeat and relax.

7. Chin tuck: Be aware of the curve of your back. Inhale straightening the back by raising your breastbone. Exhale, round the back and tuck your chin. Inhale lifting the head comfortably and straightening the back. Exhale pulling the chin into the breastbone and rounding the back. Repeat and relax.

8. Fingers & wrists: Shake your arms all the way from the shoulder opening up the armpits and down to the tips of your fingers. Wiggle the fingers and rotate the wrists one way and then the other.

9. Arms: Raise both arms above your head. Stretch upwards one arm at a time. Stretch the fingers up to grab the air above you while curling down each of the fingers separately. Stretch the other arm up grabbing the air with the fingers. Repeat with each arm. Relax.

10. Arms: Inhale raising both arms up curving the back slightly inward. Exhale slowly lowering your arms. Let your back curve outwards and your hands descend to your knees. Inhale slowly, raise your arms and exhale slowly lower your arms. Ensure the back is rounded and let your hands rest on your knees. Repeat and relax.

11. Head tilt: Put your hands on the floor beside you. Inhale, exhale tilting your head to one side, stretching the neck muscles. Hold comfortably. Inhale, raise your head, exhale tilting your head to the other side. Hold comfortably. Repeat to each side. Straighten your head and relax.

12. Eyes: Bring your awareness to your eyes. Inhale, open your eyes. Exhale and close your eyes very slowly. Soften your eyes keeping them unfocused when opening them. Repeat and then relax.

13. Take a slow breath inhaling and exhaling. Smile and repeat with 2 more breaths sitting quietly for a few minutes.

14. When you are finished and ready to stand, come up on your knees and place one foot in front, flat on the floor. Put both hands on your thigh and push up from this position.

Date & Time

_____

How do I feel?

_____

How was my day?

_____

What did I accomplish today?

_____

Did I make myself happy today?

_____

What one thing am I grateful for today?

_____

Did I meditate today?

_____

Did I enjoy my day?

_____

Did I enjoy my meals?

_____

Did I take time for myself?

_____

Am I proud of myself?

_____

STANDING POSE – STRETCHING

1. Stand comfortably, legs slightly apart, pelvis tilted slightly forward. Keep a chair close by to rest your hand on for balance. Do each of the stretches slowly and feel your body responding.

2. Toes: Become aware of your toes – all ten of them. Keep the weight evenly on the bottom of your feet and spread your toes as wide as you can and then release. Slowly curl your toes then release. Repeat each movement and then relax.

3. Feet: One foot at a time, come up on the ball of the foot and push into the floor. Release and raise the other foot pushing into the ball of the foot. Repeat and then relax both feet.

4. Knees: Without raising your heels, bend your knees and feel your calves stretching. Straighten your knees and then bend them. Repeat then relax the legs.

5. Legs: Extend the left leg to the side pointing your foot in that direction. Keep the right foot flat on the floor then bend the knee. Straighten, raise the right heel and bend the knee – be aware of the hip joint and thigh muscles moving. Bring both legs together. Repeat with the right leg extending to the side. Repeat with both legs and then relax.

6. Pelvic: Stand with feet apart and push the pelvis completely forward tightening and pulling the tummy muscles upward and curling the back outward slightly. Release and repeat. Relax the back.

7. Waist: Extend your arms straight from your shoulder area, palms facing upwards. Turn the upper body from the waist, one way comfortably sideways and then turn slowly to the other side. Repeat and then relax.

8. Shoulders: Keep the head straight and the pelvis tilted slightly forward. Inhale bending the elbows pulling them back squeezing the shoulder blade area, working the front breastbone. Exhale bringing your arms forward and hug yourself tightly feeling the back muscles stretching. Inhale bringing your elbows back again squeezing and then exhaling forward but this time reversing the arms in the hug. Repeat and then relax by letting your arms hang at your sides.

9. Neck: Drop your arms to your side, tilt your head to one side and hold for approximately 30 seconds. Raise your head slowly and tilt it to the other side and again hold for 30 seconds.

10. Chin: Raise your head and then lower your chin to your breastbone, letting the back neck and shoulder muscles stretch. Hold for approximately 30 seconds. Lower your chin diagonally to the left and hold for 30 seconds. Raise and lower your chin diagonally to the right and hold for 30 seconds. Raise your head but keep your chin slightly tucked.

11. Rib cage: Raise your arms above your head, spreading your fingers wide grabbing handfuls of air with first one hand and then the other. Stretch your arms up by raising the rib cage from the waist area each time. Lower the arms slowly and relax.

12. Waist: Raise your arms to shoulder level. Stretch the right arm to the right side bending from the waist but keep the back straight. Rock slowly to the left and stretch to the left. Keep your head straight as you do this. Repeat going back and forth to the right and then the left. Lower the arms and relax.

13. Eyes: Bring your awareness to your eyes. Inhale, open your eyes. Exhale and close your eyes very slowly. Soften your eyes keeping them unfocused when opening them. Repeat and then relax.

14. To finish, take a slow breath. Inhale and raise your arms a few inches, exhaling and lowering your arms back down to your sides. Repeat raising your arms less but lengthening your exhalation more each time.

15. Stand quietly for a few minutes and just relax.

Date & Time

_____

How do I feel?

_____

How was my day?

_____

What did I accomplish today?

_____

Did I make myself happy today?

_____

What one thing am I grateful for today?

_____

Did I meditate today?

_____

Did I enjoy my day?

_____

Did I enjoy my meals?

_____

Did I take time for myself?

_____

Am I proud of myself?

_____

BREATHING

1. When you first begin breathing exercises, you might become dizzy. Just relax and continue when you are comfortable. At first, try not to take too deep an inhalation until you get your body accustomed to it. Deeper inhalations will make you dizzy but exhalations won't. Be aware of the fact that when you begin to practice deeper inhalations, your ribs will hurt from having the muscles surrounding the ribs being stretched. This will also lessen as the muscles become accustom to the stretching.

2. You will be sitting and laying in this exercise. Bring a mat with you and a pillow for sitting.

3. Assume the sitting pose and relax a moment. Elevate your hips slightly with a book or a firm pillow. Sit with your hands in your lap palms facing upward. Keep your chin tucked.

4. Sitting bones: Sit with your back straight and slightly tilt the pelvis area. Feel the contact of your sitting bones with the surface beneath you.

5. Breath: Take a regular breath in and out through the nostrils. Repeat 2 more times. Be aware of how this feels and the depth of the breath within the chest. Be aware of the chest rising and falling with each breath.

6. Eyes: Inhale slowly and open the eyes wide. Exhale slowly and close the eyes. Repeat 2 more times. Be aware again of the chest movements.

7. Arms: Drop your arms to the side. Inhale and raise your arms slowly to shoulder level either to the side or front. Exhale and lower your arms slowly. Repeat 2 more times.

8. Back: Inhale raising your arms slowly and your head comfortably to the ceiling, arching your back inward comfortably. Exhale lowering your arms and curling your head down to your chest arching the back outward. Repeat 2 more times. Be aware of how much warmer your lungs feel with each breath.

9. Head & chest: Inhale raising your head comfortably to the ceiling and arch the back inward. Exhale slowly, keeping your head up and lowering your chest as flat as you can to your lap. Tuck the chin at the

end of the exhalation and let the arms dangle. Repeat 2 more times raising and lowering the chest.

10. Body: Lay down comfortably on the floor on a mat or warm blanket. Feel the pressure of the floor beneath your body. Inhale feeling your body expanding on the floor. Exhale feeling the pressure lessen. Repeat 2 more times, paying attention to the different contacts with the floor.

11. Arms: Extend the arms out on the floor to shoulder level. Inhale and raise the arms up palms facing. Exhale and lower the arms, palms facing outwards. Keep the back on the floor by tilting your pelvis forward – you can bring the feet flat on the floor if you want. Feel the contact of the shoulder blades with the floor opening and closing. Repeat 2 more times.

12. Knees: Keep the arms extended and bring the feet flat on the floor. Keep the pelvis tilted and the back against the floor. Inhale and exhale slowly lowering the knees to one side comfortably. Inhale, bring the knees up. Exhale lower the knees comfortably to the other side. Pay attention to the lower back and hips and the contact with the floor. Repeat 2 more times.

13. Lower the legs and assume the laying pose – legs and arms outstretched comfortably, pelvis tilted and chin tucked. Take 3 regular breaths. Be aware of the difference between the beginning regular breaths and your breath now. Be aware of the warmth in the lungs.

14. Relax a few more moments before getting up.

15. When you are finished and ready to stand up, roll onto one side and bring the knees up to hip level. Rest for a moment and put one hand flat on the floor. Push up from your hand to prevent dizziness. Come up on your knees and put one foot in front and flat on the floor. Put both hands on your thigh and push up from this position.

Date & Time

How do I feel?

How was my day?

What did I accomplish today?

Did I make myself happy today?

What one thing am I grateful for today?

Did I meditate today?

Did I enjoy my day?

Did I enjoy my meals?

Did I take time for myself?

Am I proud of myself?

STANDING POSE – BALANCING

1. Stand comfortably, legs slightly apart, pelvis tilted slightly forward. Keep a chair close by to rest your hand on for balance. Have a focal point at eye level close by.

2. Focal point: Choose an eye level focal point – a picture, word, saying, or whatever is of interest to you – something that is stable and is some feet away but easily seen.

3. Eyes: Rest your focus on your focal point. Relax the focus. Close your eyes and slowly open them gazing at your focal point each time. Repeat 2 more times. Keep your focus during the following exercises.

4. Breaths: Take 3 slow deep breaths in and out of your nostrils, lengthening each breath with each repetition.

5. Balance: Bring your feet together and let your hand rest on a secure place. Lift one foot off the floor slightly, and balance. Ensure that your balance is on the complete foot. Push the toes into the floor and feel the ball and heel of the foot. Slightly bend the heel and again balance. If you begin to wobble, continue to focus keeping the foot flat on the floor. Bring the foot down and raise the other foot. Balance, push the toes into the floor and feel the ball and heel of the foot, slightly bend the knee. Balance, focus, and bring the foot down slowly.

6. Breastbone: Lift the one foot and the opposite arm straight out to the side or front. Raise the breastbone up and keep the chin and eyes up and focused. Lower the arm and foot together then raise the other foot and opposite arm together. Balance, focus eyes and keep the breastbone raised. Lower the foot and arm together.

7. Prayer position: Lift one foot and rest it on the top of the other foot softly. Focus and lift one arm and place it at prayer position. Lift the other arm and bring the hands together and hold. Touch the breastbone softly with the side of both thumbs for extra balance. Focus and balance. If possible, close the eyes and take a slow breath. Open your eyes and lower the arms and foot. Repeat with the other foot. Be aware of the fact that you will probably be able to balance better on one foot than the other.

8. Feet: Lift one foot and raise it up a few inches above the floor in front or beside you. Raise the arms above the head or straight out at shoulder level. Balance and focus. Repeat with the other foot.

9. Body: Lift the arms up and spread the legs apart. Keep the focus. Lower the body down between the legs and keep the eyes on the focal point. Curl the head down and just hang comfortably. Raise up and lift the head by curling up and bring the eyes up to focus again as you stand up. Repeat comfortably.

10. Arms & Legs: Lift one foot and extend it out to the side while you raise both arms and spread them out wide as can be. Slowly bring your foot and wrap it around the other as much as you can. At the same time bring both arms and wrap them around your body in a big hug. Focus and balance in this position. Pay attention to which arm is uppermost. Open up and spread your leg and arms out as wide as you can. Bring your foot and arms down and then raise the other foot and both arms. Bring your foot out and your arms spread wide. Wrap your leg around the other and hug yourself with the other arm on the top reversing the original position. Hug, balance and focus. Open up and spread your arms and leg out. Bring them back to standing position and relax.

11. Prayer Position 2: Bring the legs together. Lift one foot slightly and bring the hands into prayer position in front of the breastbone. Focus and balance. Now bring your hands in front of your forehead. Again, focus and balance. Now bring your hands above your head. Focus and balance. Either release or bring the hands down to the forehead and then the breastbone, focusing and balancing each time. Repeat with the other foot.

12. Finish off by standing with feet slightly apart and pelvis tilted. Stand for a few minutes longer and just relax.

Date & Time

_____

How do I feel?

_____

How was my day?

_____

What did I accomplish today?

_____

Did I make myself happy today?

_____

What one thing am I grateful for today?

_____

Did I meditate today?

_____

Did I enjoy my day?

_____

Did I enjoy my meals?

_____

Did I take time for myself?

_____

Am I proud of myself?

_____

SITTING POSE – RELAXATION

1. Pick some soft gentle soothing music. Keep the volume lower than usual. Lower the lights and light a candle. If using scents, ensure they are not overpowering.

2. Assume the sitting pose and relax a moment. Sit on a book or firm pillow to slightly elevate your hips. Sit with your hands in your lap palms facing upward. Keep your chin tucked.

3. Back & Pelvis: Sit with your back straight by raising your breastbone and slightly tilting the pelvis area. Feel the contact of your sitting bones with the surface beneath you.

4. Listening: Listen to the soft music for a few moments. Inhale and exhale slowly through the nostrils. Be aware of your surroundings and the feeling of the room and the floor beneath you. Scan your room slowly and just be aware of colours, furniture and flooring.

5. Breathing: Bring your attention back to your breath and the music. Inhale by slowly counting 1-4 and exhale counting slowly 1-8. Repeat 2 more times lengthening the breath each time.

6. Eyes: Slowly close your eyes and rest your hands in your lap with palms facing upwards. Repeat opening and closing your eyes keeping them unfocused while open.

7. Sitting bones: As you continue to breathe slowly, rock back and forth and sideways on your sitting bones. Pay attention to the feeling of your body in contact with the floor beneath you. Come back to the center.

8. Legs: Extend your legs and shake them loosely a few times. Tense and relax the legs shaking them each time. Relax your legs and resume your sitting pose.

9. Tummy area: On your next exhalation, pull the tummy area completely in and up into the rib cage. Inhale and feel your tummy area swell with new air. Continue for a few more breaths, exhaling pulling the tummy in and then inhaling and expanding the tummy area. Relax.

10. Arms & hands: Drop your arms down and shake the arms and hands. Tense and relax the arms shaking them each time. Stop and let your arms hang. Take a complete breath and then return your hands to your lap, palms facing upwards.

11. Shoulders: Inhale raising your shoulders and feel the muscles around your ribs stretch upward and hold. Exhale dropping your shoulders gently and hold. Repeat several times.

12. Head tilt: Raise your head and inhale slowly. Exhale and tilt your head to one side. Take a complete breath while your head is tilted. Centre your head. Inhale and exhale tilting your head to the other side. Again, do a complete breath. Centre your head. Inhale and exhale dropping your chin to your breastbone. Do a complete breath and then return your head to the straight position keeping your chin slightly tucked. Take a complete breath and relax

13. To finish, become aware of the music playing softly, the soft light and any scents in your surroundings. Close your eyes and take a complete breath. Open your eyes very slowly and again take a complete breath. Sit quietly for a few moments longer before rising.

14. When you are finished and ready to stand, come up on your knees and place one foot in front, flat on the floor. Put both hands on your thigh and push up from this position.

Date & Time

_____

How do I feel?

_____

How was my day?

_____

What did I accomplish today?

_____

Did I make myself happy today?

_____

What one thing am I grateful for today?

_____

Did I meditate today?

_____

Did I enjoy my day?

_____

Did I enjoy my meals?

_____

Did I take time for myself?

_____

Am I proud of myself?

_____

WALKING MEDITATION

1. Pick a destination at least within a relaxed 10-minute walk.
2. Prepare yourself so that you will be comfortable on your walk.
3. Focus: When you are ready, focus on your destination. Think of yourself beginning your walk and ending at your destination.
4. Standing: Stand straight with a slight pelvic tilt, smile and begin your walk.
5. Awareness: Be aware of your surroundings but look towards your destination. Feel any warmth or coolness on your face.
6. Feet: Be aware of your feet comfortably striding along the earth —one foot then the other — heel then toe.
7. Leg joints: Feel your feet, ankles, knees and hips moving in unison as your leg moves forward — one then the other.
8. Arms: Feel your arms move in unison with the movement of your legs – right arm with left leg and left arm with right leg. Keep the hands comfortably open.
9. Shoulder joints: Feel the movement of your arms coming from your shoulder joints and allow your arms to swing wider and then your legs will widen their steps.
10. Head: Lift your head and look from one side to the other and notice your immediate surroundings. Do you hear birds or the breeze in the trees? What are the sounds you hear? Do you see squirrels or small animals? Does the air carry a smell? Let your senses take in nature surrounding you. Stop and be aware of anything that interests you.
11. Awareness: Be aware of the people or lack of people in your vicinity. Smile and nod at any people going by.
12. Ending: When you arrive at your destination, stop and stand still. Again, be aware of your surroundings.
13. Changing: Sit or lean against something at your destination. Change your position to let your body know you have arrived. Enjoy this time of ending.

14. Focus: When you are ready to return to your starting position, focus on it. Prepare yourself and begin again.
15. When you arrive, again sit or change position but make it an ending.
16. Begin, journey, end – define each part. Relax.

Date & Time

_____

How do I feel?

_____

How was my day?

_____

What did I accomplish today?

_____

Did I make myself happy today?

_____

What one thing am I grateful for today?

_____

Did I meditate today?

_____

Did I enjoy my day?

_____

Did I enjoy my meals?

_____

Did I take time for myself?

_____

Am I proud of myself?

_____

FINAL THOUGHTS

I hope you enjoyed the journey and doing the meditations. I still find something new every time I go over the basics. It is always a pleasure teaching new students because I relive the newness of what I do. A beautiful expression I always treasure is "to teach is to learn twice".

If you run into a time when you find things difficult, persevere and don't be hard on yourself. Begin again and enjoy the journey with a renewed sense of yourself. There is always something wonderful about beginning again and discovering new things about something that is already familiar. Obstacles come into our lives so we learn something new about ourselves.

Enjoy the journey and always take pleasure in your accomplishments.

JOURNAL NOTES

Journal Notes

Printed in the United States
by Baker & Taylor Publisher Services